ABOUT T

Orna Ross is an award-winning novelist and poet, and founder of the Alliance of Independent Authors (ALLi). Enjoying book sales in 120+ countries worldwide, she has won several awards and her work for ALLi has seen her named "one of the 100 most influential people in publishing" (The Bookseller). Born in Waterford and raised in Wexford, in the south-east corner of Ireland, she now lives and works in London and St Leonard's-on-Sea, in the south-east corner of England.

Find out more at
OrnaRoss.com

instagram.com/ornaross.poetry

FONT PUBLICATIONS IS THE PUBLISHING IMPRINT
FOR ORNA ROSS'S FICTION POETRY
AND GO CREATIVE! BOOKS.
ALL ENQUIRIES: SARAH@ORNAROSS.COM

CIRCLE OF LIFE
Inspirational Poetry for Mothers and Other Carers
E-book: 978-1-913349-00-4
Paperback: 978-1-913349-01-1
Large Print: 978-1-913349-02-8
Hardback: 978-1-913349-04-2
Audiobook: 978-1-913349-16-5

❀ Created with Vellum

ACKNOWLEDGMENTS

My thanks to Jane Dixon-Smith for cover design of this book and the *Twelve Poems to Inspire* series. To the #IndiePoetryPlease community on Instagram: thank you for writing your poems and entering the monthly prompt competition. To the publishing team: Sarah Begley, Kayleigh Brindley and Laura Park, who get the words from me to the readers. Thanks to the creators of the AI art tool Dream, app.wombo.art, through which I generate artwork from lines of the poems. To Philip Lynch, first reader and sometime muse. And most special thanks to my poetry patrons, who keep the poems coming. Your support means everything to me. With a bow, thank you all. *Sonas libh go léir.*

x Orna

CIRCLE OF LIFE

INSPIRATIONAL POETRY FOR MOTHERS AND OTHER CARERS

TWELVE POEMS TO INSPIRE
BOOK FOUR

ORNA ROSS

FontPublications

CONTENTS

INTRODUCTION

CIRCLE OF LIFE

ircle of Life is the fourth book in the *Twelve Poems to Inspire* series, compact poetry gift books for special events and life occasions. This one is for mothers, and anyone who mothers — as in, nurtures or nurses, protects or pampers —another.

As with the other books in this series, some of the poems here celebrate the beauty of motherhood but they are not all sweetness and light. Inspirational poetry pays attention to life's most elemental forces—the problematic, the challenging, even the threatening, as well as those we know to be good.

Mother love is not just the straightforward sacrifice celebrated on simple-minded greetings cards. It can be that but it is always so much more besides. Mother love is complex and mothers have huge psychic power.

Each of us was mothered into being. We are all, as the great poet Adrienne Rich put it in her book about the institution of motherhood, of woman born. But not all of us were blessed by the unconditional mother love that is so widely celebrated on greeting cards and smushy dramas.

1

When that ideal love is withheld from us, we suffer, and it's always withheld to some degree. Our mothers were and are human beings, with their own needs and flaws alongside their care for us.

The most redemptive fact about mothering is that it is a practice, as well as an experience, something we give as well as receive. Whether we are male or female, whether when growing up we had a loving or cruel mother, a neglectful mother or no mother at all, we can all, always, still mother ourselves.

And being well-mothered, by ourselves or another, is what gives us the capacity to mother those who need it.

ADVENTURES IN MOTHERING

Back in 1987, I had my first child and published my first paid article in a newspaper, in the same week. For a quarter of century afterwards, mothering and writing were intimately intertwined in my life. And still, though my children are now in their 30s, the two activities inform each other.

For me, mother is a doing word—a verb more than a noun--and writing and mothering flow from the same space. A mother nurtures an infant, a toddler, a teen and a young adult into social life, then sees them off into the world. A writer nurtures ideas and stories, rhythms and rhymes, into literary life and must then let go in a very similar way.

"I'll be there in a bit," I used to tell the children when they were small. "I'm writing now but I won't be long." At some point, I started whispering in just the same fashion to the words I had to leave unfinished in my study. "I'll be back in a bit. I won't be long."

For years, I was bemused by the roles that had arrived and claimed me. Me, a mother? Me, a writer? I didn't know which felt more unlikely but I could feel how they fed each other—how both responded well to a balance of creative work, rest and play. How both grew with a little slip back, at first, for every step forward. How both could make their own decisions and often knew more than I knew.

Both demanded that I slow down and pay attention. The American poet Mary Oliver said what we do as writers is "mostly standing still and learning to be astonished." That was my work as a mother too.

The children, though, had the capacity for astonishment, without having to remind themselves. For them the tiniest things were objects of awe, the most unlikely things were objects of play. Meal time was an elongated, messy game. A walk to the hall door with them could take an age (especially in the years when they used to attach themselves to my legs).

I could hurry them through, and be harried along, or I could go at their pace, and see with their eyes.

I must have had their capacity for wonder, as a child, but I had to relearn it as an adult writer-mother. In that relearning, I mothered a whole new layer of being into my own life.

CIRCLE OF LIFE

Mothering is always an adventure, and best embraced as such. We can't know at the beginning, in giving ourselves to a newborn, or somebody else who needs our care, what we are getting ourselves into. It's the same with a poem, as we write it, and as we read it.

Just as conception leads to birth, a sparked idea in a writer's mind births words and sentences and books. Writing, like mothering, is a profound act of creation, guidance, and emotional investment.

And so is reading. All three processes are intimate and transformative, leaving indelible marks on mind, heart and soul. The love of a good poem, just like the love of a good mother, is best received as mystery and blessing.

Poems and mothers are our inheritance. What we make of them becomes our legacy.

I hope this book fosters the embrace all kinds of mother love for you.

x Orna

CIRCLE OF LIFE

TWELVE POEMS TO INSPIRE: BOOK IV

BEGINNINGS

First Flush
The Ring
The Way of the Womb
Where Are You?

FIRST FLUSH

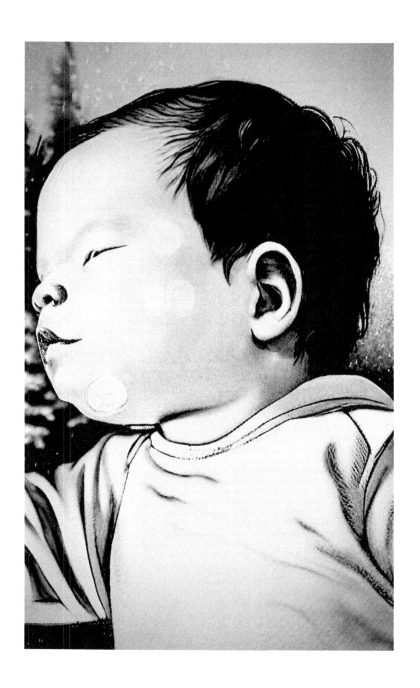

FIRST FLUSH

Not yet one day old.
As we, with your mother,
stared at the soft throb
of your vulnerable skull,

your neck so soft,
too slight, as yet, to hold
your head but already
elegant, like hers;

as we gazed with a wonder
last felt thirty years before
at your gossamer brows,
your crystalline skin,

those tiny nails, each one of ten
a pin-point of pure perfection
on your cupped feet and fingers,
the sun came out,

emerging from clouds
unnoticed until then, when
through the window sunlight
passed for the first time,

across your face,
and with you, we
were each illuminated.
All newborn.

* * *

THE RING

THE RING

From the seventeenth-century church
with the round steeple
in the centre of the town
where her mother and father married,
fifty years before,
a short walk still takes you
to the bench by the edge
of the water, where
she made her proposal.

"What a bird!" he said, that day,
and ever after, always laughing
at how she'd surprised him into it.
Down on one knee, a gold ring,
a flower for his lapel, "the works,"
as above them the church bell
started to peal. Twelve o'clock, noon.

This evening, in that place
where their candlelights were lit,
and the bell rang again at their union,
their daughter enters a cathedral of silence,
wearing their ring on a chain.

A few days before leaving home,
she was still wondering why
she needed to make this return.
Now, adrift on her bench, she is unsure
whether the flat water she watches,
is a lake or a tidal pool.
It is drawing its light from the stars,
which are beginning again

to burn themselves out
across the ceiling of sky.

The floor her bench stands on
is polished mud, and she is barefoot,
humble in her pilgrimage.
The murmur of a wave laps the shore
as she sits inside her glass bell,
holding their ring.

THE WAY OF THE WOMB

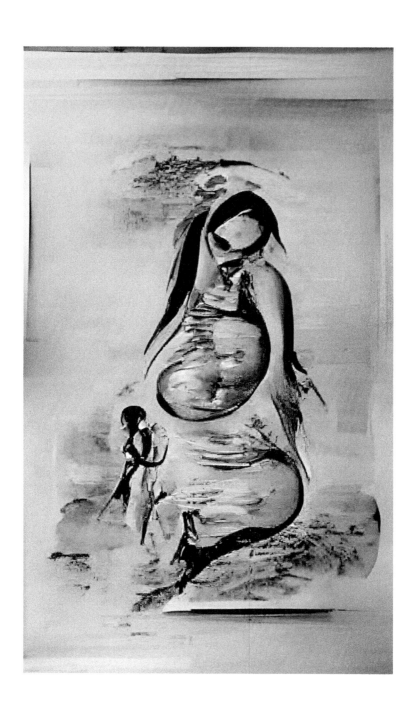

THE WAY OF THE WOMB

The people are shaken,
weakened by disease.
Now there is war in the east.
Floods to the south.
Fear stalks through the west,
dividing again our belligerent
bomb-ridden world.

No man power can save us from this.
No war words can keep us safe here.

Is it time yet? Can we let
war's thunder be our awakening?
A new seed, released? A catalyst?
What threatens us can become
our strength, if we can only know
what we want, and what's wanting.

Can we listen to the silent earth
echo, let our longing for peace
lead us to the way of the womb?

As we expand out, can we also feel in,
nurture the embryo of truth
into a swelling belly of being?

As the pains gather, insistent,
cry, as we must
(every birth is a death)
but bear down
bear down

bear down and be
the meaning delivered
from impregnation accepted.
Then, arms out, shut up and love?

WHERE ARE YOU?

WHERE ARE YOU?

The splendor of creation awaits.
Beauty veiled, she dallies,
playing with the wings
of birds passing,
swaying her hips
with the wind,
wanting to dance,
to bring you music
from planets and clouds.

Call her by right name,
hear her answer.
Male or female,
she is yours:
lingering, singing
and playing, holding out
a braceleted hand,
all tinkle and glint.

She wants to roll ecstasy
over and under your skin,
swirl bubblings into your blood,
breathe you away
through the waves of the ages.

You can stay where you are
(where are you?)
and just listen.
No, don't even listen, just be.
Unmask. That is all.

She will offer herself,
unasked and unasking.
No demands from her,
ever, to know:
where are you?

LEAVINGS

ALICE'S MOTHER

ALICE'S MOTHER

The jets spurt.
Alice gasps
as the arcs
of water gush up.
"Look Mama!"
She cries, delight
dancing her legs.
"Oh Alice, watch out!
Mind your dress!"
The jets spurt.
Alice's mother
wants to curve
her girl's soul
in the cup
of her fist.
Tuck her body
back in under
her breast.
Offset the woundings
she sees lying in wait.
The jets spurt.
Alice surveys the cascade,
then the love-worried face,
and knowing all
her mother once knew
before she grew
heavy with child,
leans in to get wet.
The jets spurt.

* * *

LOST AND FOUND

LOST AND FOUND

Inspired by **Overcoming Speechlessness by Alice Walker.** *Content Warning: paramilitary violence / murder / torture.*

* * *

Her name? Her name is Generose,
Listen to how her story flows

through the sounds of war anew,
our ruler coming out to say:
"Bombs! Again! Away!'" Through
minions mincing with regret
at what we need to do and why
evil ones must die.

Through the soldiers jumping to;
through me, and my kind, left bereft
behind, nowhere to be
except here, hoping to woo
a person like you.

Come with me. I need us to get to a place
far from here, where four or five
million...? No. Let me begin again...
Let me start here.

Yesterday. I was clearing my house.
"And not before time!" is what you
would have said if you'd seen it.
I was making two piles
– to hold or to go? -

when I found it: the book.
Lying open, face down, waiting
for me to return. I shrugged off
the me who likes to think she can
think herself safe, and picked it back up
where I'd stopped. And dropped
down again into that wood
where four million people once died.
(Or was it five?) Yes, genocide.

One mother's name was Generose,
see now how her story goes.

When they'd hear the trucks of the killers
roar in, the villagers would grab the hands
of their children and flee to the trees.
At night, they'd lie down on dead leaves,
knuckling dirt into dreams.

One day Generose and her family
were too slow to go. The soldiers
came in with machete and gun,
hacked her husband to death, then
made her climb up to lie down
on her own kitchen table,
in front of her daughter and son.
"We're hungry," they said
as they cut off her leg and sliced it
into six pieces, and fried them
up in her own pan.

Yes, name her name, it's Generose.
Listen. Listen to how it goes.

They ordered her children to partake.
The boy knew how to refuse

and was shot on the spot. The girl,
in terror, attempted to try. I ask you:
can you imagine? Not the family
so much as those soldiers,
the teaching it took to create them.

Where this happened was already famed
for kings who came from afar to take
what they would. What one liked
to take was the hands of the men
he'd enslaved, the ones who had failed
to bring in their quota of crop.
And chop them off.

* * *

Consumed by the sight of the girl
trying to force her mother
as meat through her mouth, the men
somehow allowed Generose down
from the table to crawl from the house.
And so, somehow, she survived.
And so, she has heard, did her daughter.
And so she believes that some day
she'll see her again. And she works
every which way for that day.

Why tell you all this?
May I reverse the question,
ask you how you feel when you
hear it? That's why the poet
wrote her book, though to regurgitate
that leg made her sick for weeks after.

The same choices call to us all.
Kings will do what kings do,

soldiers too, and if you don't
want to know, I won't keep you.

Let me back to the book that knows
what to own, what should be let go.
Let me wait in the place I've come
to call home, with those
who decline to oppose.

Let me hold to my hope that the girl
might be found, enfolded again,
to recollect their dead men,
that we all might recall
what we've been taught, so well,
to forget: the long-lasting hold,
the cast iron caress of the mother.

Her name, this time, was Generose,
and that is how the story goes.

* * *

TRYING

TRYING

A post-pandemic poem

We're going to town.
I try to help
but, home after years,
I don't know where
anything goes anymore.
And anyway, you say,
no need, no need.

Your outdoor shoes
are ready by the door.
Overcoat, hat, scarf:
tick, tick, tick.
Umbrella. Stick.

In town we shop,
then walk the quay
where the Slaney river
tumbles into the sea.
Walk and talk, elbows linked,
me trying not to feel
the old guilt for taking the life
you only partly permitted
me to lead.

Now you are showing me
how I will walk. And afterwards
back in the house, making tea:
how to reach gently, bend slowly,
meander around hurdles,
like the river, winding its way

through the south-east,
patient at last.
I try not to help.
I try to let you
allow us no need.

* * *

UNFIXABLE LIGHT

UNFIXABLE LIGHT

Her legs in the early morning light
are whiter than milk. Bones visible.
Wrinkles, veins, a light dusting
of hair on shin.
Swift feet that carried
her everywhere, once.
Now fearful. Thin,
papery skin, staying in.

Outside the burble of the subway,
the traffic driving through
rivers of houses and streets,
bound for eternity.
Cars make a noise
like leaves in a gale,
or the waves of an ocean,
if you don't listen too well.

A fly lands on one foot
walks along her instep
and over her toe.
She is here,
I am here,
the fly is here,
and through the window,
as morning comes in,
the stars are muting
becoming fabled again, conceding
to today's dim, unfixable light
on the edge of the Milky Way.

* * *

RETURNINGS

Blood Ocean
Source of Strength
Mother Nature
Circle of Life

BLOOD OCEAN

BLOOD OCEAN

"Come out into the garden," Mother says.
"It's almost seven and the table is laid."
Yes come. Evening wind is cooling the trees.
And look, *they* are here, whispering over the rim.

Your father stares out through the eyes
of her son. Your niece hands you a peach
with her grandfather's hands. And the young ones
chase each other, just like you and your brother,
only you two had the run of the beach
and the sea. A right pair of water babies,
your own gran used to say. Oh, those long days!
And the fire by night. And the stories they told.
Legends that were old when Homer was young.

"Yes, well," Mother says. "Now, we must eat."
We pass down the cheese, pour you some juice,
wrap a rug around your knees. Glasses are raised:
"Cheers!" And eyes meet, each to each, as *they*
breathe, for a moment upturning time.
Then retreat, as they must, on the breeze.

* * *

SOURCE OF STRENGTH

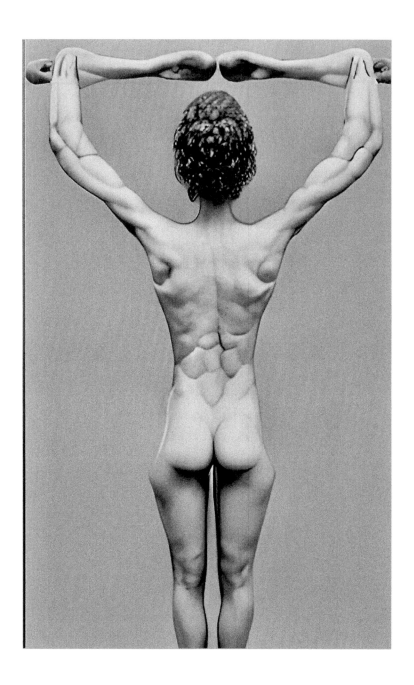

SOURCE OF STRENGTH

It is only because
she owns a once-soft skull
of separate bone plates
which only gradually fused
to allow her brain space;

an open chest
to encase the lungs
that circulate bubbles
of air in her blood,
and hold the wayward
beats of her heart in place;

a delicate pelvis
to harbour her organs
of want and waste;

and throughout her frame
the invisible power
depicted in the head of the sphinx
the gifts of the muses,
the snakes of Minoa,
the uplifted arms of Astarte,

that she can hold the weight
of this moment in her grasp,
flex her strength, and with a gasp,
bear it aloft and go to serve
the children's tea with grace.

* * *

MOTHER NATURE

MOTHER NATURE

I.
Listen, my parents,
the grasses are crawling,
the trees are thrumming,
soon birds won't be able to sing.
Listen. Hear me.
Our time is for turning.
If the old ways don't die,
we can't win.

II.
Listen, my children:
the grasses are crawling,
the trees are thrumming,
birds know what they know
as they sing. Listen...
Hear it. True time ever calling.
Lay down your despairing.
Join in.

* * *

CIRCLE OF LIFE

CIRCLE OF LIFE

...again? Are you not mother? That
is the question that must be posed
and not just to those who
work the world with their pants
less stuffed, with their arms
held aloft, when not wrapped
round the chores and the children.

No, to the big boys too, those who sooner
or later come home crying over having
to do what they had to do. Yes Sirs,
also: same question to you.

It's not just the body that moulds
and anyhow the earth that births
the him and the her of it shall,
in its time — own and good — make
a meal of our segments, slurp us up.
And, we assume, be disappeared in her turn.

Never fear. Know the question is all
that remains: how to birth? And how
to be born? Again? And again? And...

* * *

MORE POETRY INSPIRATION?

Visit my website to sign up for my monthly poetry updates and receive a free poetry book just for you. OrnaRoss.com/poetry.

Printed in Great Britain
by Amazon

29140661R00047